1637 W. Crowne: »A trve Relation of all remarkable Places and Passages observed in the Travels of the right honovrable Thomas Lord Hovvard ...«[1]

... Earle of Arundell and Surrey, Primer Earle, Earle Marshall of England, | Ambassadour Extraordinary to his sacred Majesty Ferdinando the second, Emperour of Germanie, Anno Domini 1636. | By William Crowne, Gentleman. | London, | Printed für Henry Seile [...] 1637.

herausgegeben von Norbert Flörken

---

[1] Fundstelle: BSB München; urn:nbn:de:bvb:12-bsb10469897-3; https://quod.lib.umich.edu/e/eebo/A19674.0001.001/1:3?rgn=div1;view=fulltext. Siehe https://kaiserin.hypotheses.org/702.

Zur Textgestaltung:

Rechtschreibung und Zeichensetzung sind beibehalten worden, gegebenenfalls sind Namen in der modernen Schreibweise hinzugefügt worden. Die Punkte hinter den einfachen Zahlen, z.B. den Jahreszahlen, sind weggelassen worden. Der Text der Vorlage steht in dieser Serifenschrift, Zusätze und Ergänzungen des Bearbeiters in dieser serifenlosen Schrift. Die Klammern der Vorlage ( ) sind durch { } oder – – ersetzt worden. Streichungen des Herausgebers stehen in ( ), Ergänzungen in [ ]. Fremdsprachige Wörter und Zitate sind *kursiv* gesetzt. Beim Seitenwechsel wurde die anfallende Trennung aufgehoben. Die häufigen Sperrungen bei Eigennamen oder Ortsnamen wurden nicht übernommen. Die Angaben zu Personen, Orten oder Sachen sind dem Portal Wikipedia entnommen.

Impressum

Bibliographische Information der Deutschen Nationalbibliothek:
Die Deutsche Nationalbibliothek verzeichnet diese Publikation in der Deutschen Nationalbibliographie, detaillierte bibliographische Daten sind im Internet über http://dnb.dnb.de abrufbar.
© Norbert Flörken
Herstellung und Verlag:
BoD – Books on Demand, Norderstedt
ISBN 9783749406791

9 783749 406791

Inhalt

[Preface]

To the true noble and my honourable Master, Master Thomas Hovvard, Sonne and Heire to the Right Honorable Henry Lord Matravers, Grandchilde to the Right Honorable Thomas Earle of Arundell and Surrey, Lord high Marshall of England, and his Majesties late Ambassadour to the Emperour of Germany.

Noble Sir, I know your intinate goodness is such, that you cannot contemne this well intended Abstract, though gathered by an infirme hand, considering, it reporteth the difficult Embaßie of no lesse person than your most ennobled Grandfather, my dred Lord, from whose sage steps, when our King shall please to invite you, to give <> Caesar a second visit, you may the better know the way, and be secured from many imminent dangers by such a provident care : pardon me, deare Sir, that I make your choice tendernesse my Patron {since the Discourse is no more pleasing} my aimes and endeavours beaing all bent to serve you ; and therefore the effects must needs by yours : truly Sir, your early beginnings promise such a rare proceeding, that you seeme to anticipate your age by out-stripping time in your wisedome ansd sweet discretion, And if I may obtaine your beloved smiles in this bold, though honest, action, I shall not feare what the sharpe jerke of any malignant tongue can doe unto me, but will glory in my Character, Happy Servant in such a Master,

William Crowne.

< >

A Relation by way of Journall, etc.

The seventh of April being Thursday, 1636[2], His Excellency departed from Greenwich for Germanie, tooke Barge about three of the clocke in the morning, and landed at Gravesand, from hence by Coach to Canterbury to bed, the next day to Margate where we dined, and about three of the clocke in the afternoone, hee tooke shipping in one of the Kings Ships called the ›Happy Entrance‹, and

---

[2] Crowne rechnet – wie damals alle Angehörigen der Anglikanischen Kirche – nach dem Julianischen Kalender, nach dem heute gültigen Gregorianischen Kalender ist es der 17. April. Dementsprechend sind auch die folgenden Daten umzurechnen.

landed the tenth day being Sunday at Helver sluce, and from trence to the Brill, there sailing over a lake into Masans sluce [=Maas Sluis], and so on by waggons to Delph, and to the Hage, but a mile before wee came thither, there met us some of the Queene of Bohemia's Coaches, which her Majesty sent for his Excellency, and in one of them his Excelleny went to her Majesty that night, the time we staid there, was spent in visits betweene the Prince of Orange,

<2>

his Excellency and the States[3], with some other Ambassadours, that were then there, as the French, Venetian, and the Swedish, heere we staid three daies, and departed the fourteenth day by wagons, passing through Leiden to Woerden, and then entred the Bishopricke of Utrecht, and so to the City it selfe where wee lay, the Princes being there at schoole, his Excellency went to see them that night, the next day thence to Rhenem to dine, where the Queene hath an house adjacent to the Rhine, on the left side, which wee viewed, having faire roomes and gardens

---

[3] D.i. die niederländischen Generalstaaten.

belonging to it, after diner, wee entered into Gelderland, so through Wagening to Arnheim to bed, passing that afternoone through much danger, by reason of Out-lyers from the Army at Schenckenschans, which was not farre off, the Prince of Brandeburgh being heere in Towne, visited his Excellency the next day, and the day after his Excellency visited him, who was shewed by him, the ashes of some Romanes preserved in pots, that were found in a Mountaine called Zanten, which wee afterward passed by, heere wee lay Easter-day and the Monday following, and did see the smoake and fire out of the great Peeces from the Sconce, as they were in skirmish, thether his Excellency sent the Steward and a Trumpeter to demand passage of the Spanyard in the Schans, and Grave William for the Hollander, but the Spaniard would not grant it, without order from Brussels, Grave William hearing their answer, sent his Excellency word, hee made no doubt, but to give him free passage the next day, for he resolved to make an assault that night upon the Sconce, upon the assault, the Spaniards yeelded it up on conditions, and heere

<3>

his Excellency published certaine orders, to be generally observed amongst us, one reason was, the sickenesse, being heere very much, wee staid heere three daies and departed the nineteenth in waggons for the Schans, first crossed over the Rhine just by the towne on to the right side into Cleveland, and so to the Tolhouse, a Castle where the Hollander stake toll at, adjoyning to the Rhine on the same side, then passing through all their workes and Army, leaving the Schans at a distance which was miserably battered, untill wee came to Grave William his Tent, where some of the Spaniards were sealing of their agreements what quarter they should have, who instantly left them, to bring bis Excellency over the Rhine on a Bridge of flat bottom'd Boates, guarded with all his Troopes of Horse, untill wee came at the Barke wherein his Excellency lay that night, then returned and sent a Company of English Souldiers to guard it, the next day earely wee weighed Anchor and sailed up the Rhine, having a Guard of Souldiers along the shore, by reason the Enemy went out of the Schans that morning, so passing by Emmerick and Rees, Townes with strong sconces adjoyning to the

Rhine on the left side, then in sight of the Mountaine Zanten on the other side, so by Burick, on the same side, to Wesell a Towne on the left side of the Rhine, against which wee cast Anchor, and lay on ship-board all night, for they died there of the sickenesse more than thirty a day, neverthelesse the next morning we tooke waggons in number eighteen and displaied our English colours in three severall wagons, passing over a little River in Boats call'd Lipp, then by Rheinbergh on the right hand being the last

<4>

Towne of the States, then by Dinslacken, on the same side to Dinsburgh to dinner, where none of our carriage might enter in, for as his Excellency entered the gate, one of the watch discharged his peece neere unto the horses breast, the rest being instantly commanded to the contrary, but the Gates were shut up, and wee kept out, untill the Towne were satisfied, wee were no Enemy, our carriage and Company being great, frightened them at the first after diner we past through a long VVood in much danger, and in the view of Rogues, who did not set upon us because our Company was great, yet we fearing the worst, hadm sent for a Convoy of Musketiers to the next Towne before, who met us not untill we were out of the VVood.

Then wee entered into Bergish-land, and went by Keiserswert to Dusseldorp to bed, which adjoynes to the Rhine on the left side, where the Duke of Neinburgh lay, who was with his Dutchesse abroad taking the aire, but espying us comming, returned backe into the Towne with speed, and sent to have the Ports shut up, thinking wee had beene some Enemy, but hearing it was his Excellency, was very joyfull, and sent Coaches for him, to come and suppe with him and to make ms house his lodging the time he staid, but we next morning after breake-fast, perceiving his Excellency would goe away, had three Coaches waiting at the doore, into one hee put his Excellency, and us into the rest, and brought us out of Towne, with a Company of Horsemen and Foote in Armes, and a Troope of Lances going before, and Trumpets sounding about the Coach, his owne Guard being thus brought without the Gates, hee tooke his leave of his Excellency,

<5>

and returned, and as wee were departing, there went off great peeces of Ordnance.

Thence neere Neusse, and then crossed over the Rhine at a little Dorpe called Hittorpe, into the Territory of Collein, and then to the City where we lay. It is seated on the right side of the Rhine, where the Bishop of Mentz was, who sent one of his Privie Counsell to invite his Excellency the next day to diner, he then lent three of his Coaches for us, and gave his Excellency very noble entertainement; the first night his Excellency came, were presented unto him twenty foure Flaggons of severall kindes of Wine, the next day twenty eight, and at every Present, there was a long speech made to his Excellency in Latine by one that came with the Wine, which came all from the Magistrates of the City in Flaggons with the City Armes on them, the Jesuits there have built them a very stately Church and richly adorned it with gildings and erected an Altar one of the stateliest, I ever saw, in the City likewise there is a great Church called the Dome, wherein lye the Bodies of three Kings, called The three Kings of Collein, which went to worship our Saviour, then is there another Church called

Saint Ursulas, in which lyeth the bones of 1100[4] Virgins in places locked up, and Saint Ursula in a faire Tombe by them, which came all thither with her for their Devotion, there is besides a Nunnery and some English Nunnes there.

Heere we staid a weeke, and the twenty eighth day wee tooke a Boate drawne with nine horses and went up the Rhine, by many Villages pillaged and shot downe, and many brave Vineyards on Mountaines,

<6>

along the Rivers side, passing by Bonn on the right side and seven high Burghens with old Castles on them, seated on the other side of the River, and to Drachenfels Castle on the left of the Rhine, against which wee cast Anchor and lay that night on ship-board, the next morning earely weighed Anchor, passing by an Island in which is a Monastery of Nunnes called Nonenwerther, so on by Hammerstein Castle by Keigrmagen, Andernach and Ormus three Townes on the right side of the Rhine, against Ormus wee cast Anchor and lay on ship-board.

---

[4] Die Legende spricht von 11.000 Jungfrauen.

The next day earely weighed Anchor and went by
Engers on the left side, and there begunne Trierischlandt,
and so to Coblentz a Towne adjoyning to the Rhine on
the right side, which the French lately lost, being driven
out by the Emperours Forces into a Castle seated on a very
high Rocke, opposite to the Towne called Hermanstein
[=Ehrenbreitstein], which commandeth the Towne, who
were then skirmishing when wee came, wherefore wee cast
Anchor about halfe an Engliah mile before, and sent a
Trumpeter desiring passage, which they willingly granted,
ceasing their fight on both sides, the Generall in the
Towne making preparation to entertaine his Excellency,
did but open the Gate, thinking to cleare the passage for
his Excellencies entrance, presently they in the Castle let
flye a Cannon and were like to have slaine some of them,
wherefore they withdrew from shewing of themselves, untill his Excellency came against the Gate, and then came
forth and intreated his Excellency to dine with him, but
hee staid not having a long way to goe that night, they in
the Castle are besieged on

<7>

every side, before them are Cannons placed just by the Rivers side, behinde them are a great company of Horsemen called Crabbats, beyond them in a plaine great field, are other Horsemen and Footemen, and likewise in Islands in the Rhine, all watching that they cannot be relieved, they in the Towne, if they doe but looke out of their windowes, have a bullet presently presented at their heads, yet the Towne is somewhat the stronger for a River called the Mosell, which runneth along one side of the Towne into the Rhine, over which there did stand a faire Bridge, though part of it now be beaten downe, that there is no passage over, but have made a little lower on the Mosell a passage on Boates, to relieve the Towne, under the Castle there is a very beautifull house, which the Emperour gave to the Elector of Tryer, and hee resigned it to the French, whereupon the Spaniard besieged him, when he lay in a faire Castle on the Mosell called Tryer, and tooke him prisoner, and is prisoner now: as wee were departing from hence, the French gave us a brave vollie of shot as hath beene heard, with foure or five peeces of Ordnance, from hence up the Rhine, by Lonstein and Branbach two

Townes on the left side, and Capelle a Castle on a Rocke on the other side, to Boppart a Towne on the same side, against which wee cast Anchor and lay aboard.

The first of May being Sunday, and their Whitsunday, we departed, passing by Villages shot downe, and by many pictures of our Saviour and the Virgin Mary, set up at the turnings of the water, untill we entered the Land of Hesse, where we still viewed pleasant Vines on the Mountaines, so by Saint Geware [=Goar], and

<8>

by Rheinfilds Castle both on the right side, to Catzenelbogon Castle on the other side, then by Oberwesell on the right side, then begins the Lower Palatinate, so by Caub on the left side, which is the first Towne in the Pfaltz, and so to Pfaltz Castle, seated in a little Iland in the River, from hence to Bacbarach, a Towne where we landed, it is seated on the right side of the Rhine, having a Castle on a high Rocke within the walls, and under that a Church, which is from the plaine ground 100 steps before one can come into it, heere the poore people are found dead with grasse in their mouthes: from hence by a Village on the same side, in which none but Leapers are, being not farre off the Towne, and so to Hambach on the same side, by Drechshausen on the other side, to Asmanshausen, a Towne on the left side of the Rhine, against which we cast Anchor and lay on Ship-board.

The next morning departed hence and then begun Montzistzland, so by a little Tower in the water, called Mouse Thour, which one Otto a Bishoppe of Mentz, having lived not well, being much troubled with Mice, built this, and lived in it, thinking there to be secure, but even thither they pursued him also, and eate him up: then by Bingen, a faire Towne on the right side, and by Ehrenfels Castle on the other side to Rudesheim, a Towne on the left side of the Rhine, into which I entered, and did see poore people praying where dead bones were in a little old house, and here his Excellencie gave some reliefe to the poore which were almost starved as it appeared by the violence they used to get it from one another: from thence by Geisenheim, Elfeld, and Wallaff, three Townes

<9>

on the left side of the River, and then we crossed over the Rhine, unto the other side.

Then to Mentz a great City seated close by the Rhine on the right side against which wee cast Anchor and lay on ship-board, for there was nothing in the Towne to relieve us, since it was taken by the King of Sweden, and miserably battered, there the King of Bohemia dyed, in a faire corner house towards the Rivers side, heere likewise the poore people were almost starved, and those that could relieve others before, now humbly begged to bee relieved, and after supper all had reliefe, sent from the Ship ashore, at the sight of which they strove so violently, that some of them fell into the Rhine and were like to have bin drowned.

The next day being the third of May, from hence wee departed, leaving the Rhine halfe a league above the City on our right hand, and entered into a shallow River called the Maine, passing by a place which the King of Sweden was building for a Fort, but could not finish it, then by Cassell, on the left side, thence by Flersheim on the left side to Russelsheim on the right of the Maine, and then to the stately City of Francfort, adjacent to the Maine on the left side, where we landed and lay: from Collein hither, all the Townes, Villages, and Castles bee battered, pillaged or burnt, and every place wee lay at on the Rhine on ship-board, we watched, taking every man his turne; heere wee staid foure daies, untill our carriages were made ready: where we saw the place wherein they keepe the Dyet, af-terward entered into the Church called Saint Bar-tholmews, where the Emperours use to bee crowned and take their oath; the City is inhabited with Lutherans

<10>

and Iewes, for in the Iewes Synagogue, I entered in to see the manner of their service, which is an undecent way, miking a hideous noise, having on their heads and about their neckes things called Capuchins, the women are not admitted into their Synagogue, but in places about. And on Sunday the seventh of May, by waggons through the City over two Bridges which are alwaies guarded with Souldiers, leaving the Maine on our left hand, from hence we tooke a Convoy of Musketiers along, being wee went through much danger, by Offenbach, Selgenstat, seated betweene us and the Maine, passing thus along through a great Forest in much danger, hearing the great Peeces so swiftly discharge off at Hannaw, which the Swedes subdu'd, and now besieged by the Emperors Forces, being not above three English miles off, then by a very great Mountaine two English miles long, all beset with Vines, untill we came at a poore little Village where wee staid and dined with provision of our owne, and after dinner departed, passing through Plaines untill wee came at the Maine, and there ferried over into a towne called Klingenberg, passing through this, we came to a very high hill the way up being all stone & 2 English miles up to the top, and then through a Wood, after we were past this, we came to a poore little Village called Neunkirchen, where we found one house a burning when we came and not any body in the village, heer we were constrained totally all night, for it grew very late, and no Towne neere by 4 English miles, spending the night in walking up and downe in feare, with Carrabines in our hands, because we heard Peeces discharg'd off in Woods about us, and with part of the coles of the consumed house

<11>

his Excellency had his meat rosted for supper, the next morning earely, his Excellency went to view the Church, which we found rifted with the pictures and Altars abused, in the Church-yard, we saw a dead body scraped out of the grave, in another place out of the Church-yard, there lay another dead body, into many of the houses wee entered, and found them all empty. From this miserable place we departed, and heard after, that they in the Village fled by reason of the sicknesse, and set that house on fire at their departure, that Passengers might not be infected.

Then came we into Wijrtzburg-land , and descended downe another steep hill and there crossed over a little River call'd Tauber, and through Keichelsheim to Neubruim a poore Village where wee dined, after dinner passing by the side of the Maine and through Woods and Plaines, untill we came to Wijrtzburg, a faire City passing over a bridge first, standing over the Maine into the Towne, seated on the left side of the River, and a faire Castle opposite to the Towne on the other side, in which the Towne put all their riches when they heard the king of

Sweden was comming, thinking there it would not be gain'd, but they hearing of it, surprised and pillaged it in 3 daies, and it was 3 or 4 moneths before the Emperors forces could regaine it, the next day earely departed, being the 10th of May, and entered Margrafen-land, and to Kitzingen to diner, after diner, thence through Ipza a City, and so to Marckbibrach, where we lay all night on the plancher, for the Village was pillaged but the day before, earely the next morning wee went away and passed through Neustadt, which hath beene a faire City, though now pillaged

<12>

and burnt miserably, heere we saw poore children sitting at their doores almost starv'd to death, to whom his Excellency gave order for to relieve them with meat and money to their Parents, from hence we went to Eilfkirchen a poore Village where wee dined, wich some reserv'd meat of our owne, for there was not any thing to be found, after diner, thence we passed by many Villages pillag'd and burnt down, and so into Nurnbeger-land, passing through the place where the King of Swedens Leaguer lay, when the King of Bohemia was with him and my Lord Craven, in sight of the place the Emperors Army had intrenched themselves by the side of a great wood, here the King of Sweden set upon poles alive three of his fouldiers, for killing 2 of their Commanders, and flying presently to his Enemy, and at the end of a Battaile that was then fought, he tooke them prisoners, and so executed them, then drawing neere Nurnburg a great City seated in a Plaine, which the King of Sweden relieved at that time against the Emperor, being not above two English miles off, heere we passed by some of their workes before the Towne, and then entered the Gate into the City being very stately built, and one of the strongest in Germany; and so to his Excellencies lodging, the next day the Lords of the City came and visited his Excellency; here we laid 11 daies untill his Excellency had word for certain where the Emperor was, the most part of our time was spent in seeing of the rare things in the Towne, as a very brave Magazine wherein all their munition lieth, which the Governours of the towne shewed his Excellency, at our first entrance wee passed through a large Court where there lay on our left hand 4 great Cannons by

<13>

the walles side, which were 6 paces long, and 2 foote broad, and worke-houses there likewise, then entered we into a long roome where there hung on both sides armour for foot and horse, and then into the place it selfe, where there were 6 partitions each 28 paces long and 6 broad, all full of brasse Peeces and other small ones of severall rare inventions, from hence we went to see a very rare water-worke which supplieth all the City, adjoyning close to the wall of the Towne, returning homewards, we entered into their great Church call'd the Dome, there his Excellency was shewed a very lately picture of the Annunciation of the Virgin Mary, which hung in the middle of the Quire, drawne up, which had not bin shewed to any in 18 yeeres before, and then returnd home, and the Lords with him, who supped with his Excellency, the next day they dined with him likewise, and after diner desired his Excellency to goe and take the aire in some of their Gardens without the City, which he did: the City is very strong being encompassed without the wals with bulwarkes and a mighty deepe and wide ditch, and within are many curiosities and stately buildings: the ancient men {called Lords} governe by turnes not acknowledging any particular Prince their Soveraigne, but hold correspondency with all, for in the time of those great wars between the Emperor and the King of Sweden, they would resigne to the Emperor one while, and to the K. another, paying great taxes & impositions to their halfe undoing. From hence we departed May 22. being Sunday, for Regenspurgh, thinking there to meete with the Emperor, first passing through a part of the upper Palatinate, to Newmark, where we lay, seated in a plaine where the king of

<14>

Bohemia had a house, which his Excellency viewed, adjoyning to the wall within the Towne, fortified with bulwarkes and pallizadoes, having spacious roomes and a faire Armory: early the next morning from hence, by Churches demolished to the ground and through Woods in danger, understanding that Crabbats were lying heere about, untill we came at a poore little Village called Hemmaw where

24

we staied and dined, which hath beene pillaged eight and twenty times in two yeeres, and twice in one day, and they have there no water but that which they save when it raineth: after dinner, to Esserhausen a poore Village where we crossed over a little River in Boates, the Bridge being burnt downe by the Swedes forces; from hence wee ascended up a high hill, being descended downe, wee passed a long on an high banke, having the River Danubius on our right hand, and high Mountaines with Vines on our left, passing thus through severall Villages beaten downe or burnt, untill we came at a round Fort before the Bridge which a guard kept, and so over it through a Tower in the middle standing over the Danuby, which runneth with as swift a current as at London Bridge, dividing it selfe into severall Ilands which have had howses on them, but now burnt, and also houses on the Arches which were demolished likewise, then into the Citie Regenspurg to his Excellencies lodging, the Citie hath bin taken by Swedish forces, and regained by the King of Hungary.

The 25. day his Excellency went to take the ayre on the other side of the Towne, and as we went did see the ruines of many houses and Churches, and one Carthusian Monastory so much ruinated as the rest, into

<15>

which his Excellency entered to see the roomes wherein the King of Hungary did lie all the time hec was regaining of the Citie, being not above two English miles off it, and heere likewise the old Duke of Bavaria, this Dukes Father lived in a Cell for many yeers together, againe his Excellency went to take the ayre the 28. day, and entered into a Jesuites Monastery, in which there is one Altar dedicated to S. George; here his Excellency staied a weeke, and departed thence for Lintz, where the Emperour was, taking foure Boates and went downe the Danow thorough Bavaria, passing by a Castle called Donastauff, seated on a high Mountaine, with a Dorpe at the foote of it, adjoyning to the Danubiij on the left side, and by Werth Castle on the same side, to Straubingen on the same side where we landed about eleuen at night and lay that night; the next morning from thence, still by many ruines to Pogen on the right side, at the foote of a very high Mountaine, and on the top of it a Church with a few houses about it; then by

Nuternberg Castle seated on a high Mountaine on the right side of the River, and by Deckendorff on the other side, against which wee met with thirty horses fastened all to one rope drawing of sixe great boats which were going to Regenspurg, then by a Castle called Tawrino seated on a high Mountaine, and below at the bottome is a Towne called Overwinter on the left side, and so to Vilshoven, a, towne on the right of the Danunby where wee landed and lay that night. The next morning as his Excellency was taking Boate, he spied a poore Boy standing among other poore people begging for reliefe, who looked very strangely and could neither speake nor heare, but a

<16>

little at his mouth and nofe, having neither eares nor passage to heare with, and his face very thin & drawne aside, yet when one hallowed hee heard and answered againe with a noise, there was with him his sister, a pretty girle, who when one spake to him, made him understand by lignes, these two his Excellency tooke along with him in his Boate to a City called Passaw on the right side of the Danuby, where we landed & lay, and there commanded to have new clothes made for them & gave them monie and sent them home to their freinds, and a little before we came thither, endeth Bavaria; this Citie is seated very sweetly, having 3 rivers running neere it, the Danuby which is of a green color, incompasseth it of one side, and a swift river called Inn, on the other side, which commeth out of Italy, and is of a white color, the third is Ilze, which is very blacke, and commeth out of Bohemia, and both runne into the Danuby at the end of the towne, the next day his Excellency went to view a Capuchine Monastery, seated very pleasantly on a high hill, heere unto the Towne, first we passed over a bridge made of little rafts which standeth over the river Inn, and so through Instadt, and then ascended up the hill upon which the Monastery stands, and then entered into the Chappell called our Ladies Chappell, being built in the yeere 1636, where we saw a neat Altar, and a picture of the Virgin Maries set up in the Altar, and many fine reliques, left there of those that are said to have been healed of severall diseases, comming but thither to doe their Devotion, and returned thence sound, from hence we descended to another Chappell at the bottome of the hill, passing downe 274 steps, being set in order, 10 and 11 together.

<17>

And as much plaine ground as containeth the steps thorow out the whole descent, and in the middle of the descent is a Crucifix, at which one daily sits to receive the almes of charitable people, which Crucifix one rude person passing by, strucke it, and fell downe dead and never revived, as these Capuchines related, and then returned. And opposite to the citie on the other side of the Danuby on a very high rocke, is seated a strong Castle which cannot be scaled, called Festingoverhouse, commanding all the Townes and Monasteries; at the foot of this is another strong built Fort, by which the river Ilze falleth into the Danuby, betweene the towne Ilze and this: the citie is governed by Leopoldus the Emperours second sonne, who is Bishop of it; here we stayed three dayes, and departed the fourth of Iune, and entred into upper Austria, passing by Schaumberg castle on the left side of the river, and by Effertingen on the other side, and Wilhering Monastery on the same side, to Lintz where the Emperour was, who sent

to receive his Excellence at his landing the Count of Har-
rack, Marshall of the Court, with some other Courtiers;
after his gratulation with his Excellence, there came ten or
twelve coaches, which waited on his Excellence to his
lodging which the Emperour had provided, and then returned. Presently after came the Count Megaw, high
Steward to the Emperour, to visit his Excellence; and the
next day Count Mansfelt Captaine of the Foot-Guard to
visit his Excellence, and after him Father Lemmarman, his
Majesties Confessour.

The sixth of Iune, being the second day after wee came,
his Excellence had audience of the Emperour

<18>

and Empresse, who sent their coaches for us; being
come to his palace, which is seated on a hill, we went up
foure ascents of staires, the Guard standing on each side
of us, with halberds and carrabines in their hands, passing
thus thorow roomes, untill wee came at the doore of the
chamber in which the Emperour was, and when his Excellence came at the doore, out came the little Count of
Kezell, high Chamberlaine to his Majestie, and brought in

his Excellence, and then withdrew and shut the doore after him, that none might enter in: after his Excellence had beene within a while, we were all admitted, and kissed his Majesties hand, and then withdrew, and passed thorow other roomes and a gallerie, where the Guard stood in like manner, to the Empresses chamber, where none might enter neither, stealing a sight of her as wee stood, and then returned.

The eighth day his Excellence had his second audience of the Emperour, as private as the first: and the tenth day audience againe of the Empresse, and then wee were admitted to kisse her hand: the same day there were seven men beheaded which were Rebels, for rising up in armes with foure hundred other Boores against the Emperour: the first that was executed, was said to be one that had inchanted himselfe, that no bullet could hurt him, and the onely seducer of the others: after he was upon the scaffold and his face covered, two men held him fast to the blocke, then came the Executioner with a red hot paire of pincers, and violently clapt hold of both his brests, that done, nailed his right hand fast to the blocke, and chopt it off, then presently whipt out his sword from

<19>

his side, and cut off his head, one of the hangmen presently tooke it up, and cryed at the eares of the head, Iesus, Iesus; then the Iesuite which came a long with him admonishing of him, desired everie one to joyne in prayers with him for him; then came the other, and a Boy which was beheaded likewise, all making their private confessions to Priests, at the foot of the scaffold, having a Crucifix in their hand, kissing their hands & feet at the end of everie prayer: After all those men were beheaded, and quartered, there went two of their confederates a foot to bee hanged about an English mile off, to a place where a Priest of theirs hung upon a pole, and his head on the top, which was taken in a Church a yeere before called Ering, which we afterward passed by.

The twelfth day being Sunday, the Emperour, Empresse, and the Arch-Dutchesse, dined at the Iesuites College; but before, they heard Masse in their Church, and after dinner a play was presented to them by the house, and some young schollers, consisting of many varieties. The fifteenth day his Excellencie dined at the Count Meg-aws, and was nobly entertained: the sixteenth day as we were at dinner, there came a mightie clap of thunder and lightning, which burnt downe three houses presently, be-ing not above an English mile off, on the other side of the water, and such accidents happen here often, by reason all their houses be covered with thin boord, in the manner of tile; and about foure of the clocke in the after-noone, his Excellence had audience the third time, and we all invited to a Balto, by the Empresses command, to the Count Slav-ataes, who is Chancellour of Prague, where

<20>

all the Ladies assembled, and there spent the time in dancing: in Moravia not farre from this place, there was a Baron whose name was Rabell, having a wife, which cou-ple had beene married fortie yeeres together, and had many children, and when he was eightie two yeeres old, and his wife seventie five, she conceived and brought him forth two children at a birth, a sonne and a daughter, which children lived a yeere and died, and then presently after their parents both died, and was buried in S. Michaels Church, a Church of the Dominicans in Brune, a towne in Moravia: this storie was related to us by a Priest of the Empresses for certaine; here his Excellence stayed nineteene dayes, and all the time at the Emperours charge, and served by his Majesties servants, in as much state as he himselfe; at the first course the Drums beat up, and at the second, musike with voyces.

From hence we tooke boat for Vienna, the three and twentieth day of Iune, passing downe the swift river Danuby, neere the Church called Ering, wherein the Boores assembled and chose that Priest, who was taken and executed as afore-mentioned, so by a faire castle called Spiulbarke, where the Duke of Bavaria makes his Toll-place seated on the left side of the river, then by Markhawsen on the same side, by Walzig a faire castle seated on the other side on a high hill, and the towne at the foot a little beyond, so by another faire castle called Crayne, seated on a high rocke close by the Danuby, on the left side, the towne at the foot of it, both belonging to the Count Megaw: then thorow a place in the water called the

Struddell, where it runneth very swift, with a great fall amongst the rockes,

<21>

and dangerous to passe, having no more space than the breadth of a boat, which if it toucheth, breakes into many peeces, and over this place on a high rocke is a Crosse set up, having past this danger, just by on the left side of the River is an old Chappell called S. Nicolas, out of which came two men with his picture in a box, to receive an ac-customed reward due from those which passe by safe: from hence by a faire castle called Besinboe, seated on the same side on a rocke, and by Pekelem on the same side, then by Wednick castle seated on a rocke on the left side, with a village beneath it, so by a castle and monasterie encircled with a wall, seated on a verie high rocke called Milke, and the towne at the foot of the rocke along by the Danuby on the right side, part of it burnt by an accident when the King of Hungary was in it, and by Sable castle on a high rocke on the same side, with a faire banquetting house, which belongeth to the Grave Sturbutz; and a little further on the same side, is another banquetting-house, called the

Devils banquetting-house, by reason of many apparitions there seene. Then to a little poore Dorp called Aspagh on the left side of the Danuby, where wee went a shore and lay that night.

Earely the next morning, being the foure and twentieth day, we went up the river by a castle called the Spitz, seated on the same side, so by Stiringsteine, a faire towne on a rocke adjoyning to the river on the same side, with a ruinated castle over the towne on a hill, with rocks on both sides, which are the Grave Van Seldingz: then by another faire towne seated on the same side called Stine, from which there standeth a

<22>

bridge over the Danuby made of rafts, having thirtie seven arches, under which wee passed, and at the end of it, opposite to the towne is a monasterie with many faire houses belonging to it, and behinde this is another stately built monasterie, called Kitne, seated on a hill: from this an English mile distance, with a delightfull prospect, just by are two other faire townes, the one Crempz, and the other Winsell, seated both on the left side of the Danuby in a plaine, which three townes are within the compasse of an English mile; then by Tolnie a towne on the other side, which is the oldest towne in all the Empire, against which wee lay a while and dined on ship-boord: after dinner wee entred into lower Austria, and went by an old castle called Griffopsteine, seated on a rocke on the same side, in which all Priests that offend are imprisoned and tried.

Then a Dutch mile further, on the left side, the Danubius runneth out to a faire Towne called Cornybrough, seated an English mile off in a Plaine with faire Monasteries therein, then on the other side of the river is Cloysternybrough, full of Cloysters and Monasteries; so by Nustorffe on the same side, from whence we discovered Vienna, seated in a Plaine, then left the Danu, which divides its selfe into sever all branches and meet beyond the Towne, and runs thorow Hungary into the blacke Sea, and went up in an arme of it to the Citie, where wee landed, seated on the right side of the Danu, which is very well fortified round the wals, besides a compleat Regiment of 1500 men alwayes ready in armes, part watching at everie gate, some about the Emperours palace, others about

<23>

the place where the Iewes keep their shops in the Citie, for they are not suffered to lye in the Towne a night, but constrained to keepe within a place on the other side of the River opposite to the Citie, which they have built, and is called the Iewes Burg; for if any one be found all night in the Towne, he is miserably punished, if not put to death: there are likewise 7.000 Burgers in the citie, which are to be in armes at an houres warning.

The next day being Sunday, his Excellence had audience of the Queene of Hungary and the Arch-Duke Leopoldus, the Emperours second sonne, being the 26. day, and nothing wee saw note-worthy at his palace, but a spacious Court-yard: the next day againe his Excellence went to see the Dukes lodging, where we saw onely a few pictures; from hence he went to severall houses of the Iesuites, the first was a University, where was presented to his Excellence a kinde of Comedy by young Schollers in masking attire, and one of the house playing on an instrument like a Virginall, severall kindes of musicke; after that, a banquet brought in by the Actors: this ended, we went to the second house called the Probation-house, where none but young men are, about fiftie in number, there to be tried whether they may bee made capable of holy orders: thence to the third house, called the Profest-house, where none but the ancient Fathers are, where as soon as his Excellence entred, an oration was made to him by one of the chiefe, & after viewed the house and Church, in which there was an hymne sung by their best singers, with very sweet musicke, and they have an organ of five thousand pipes. From hence

<24>

wee returned home to our lodging, where there came presently after the Prince of Ducardins to visit his Excellence.

The eight and twentieth day his Excellence went to see a garden of the Emperours about a Dutch mile off, called Nigobath, upon which place the Turke once intrenched himselfe, when hee would have taken Vienna, and was then two hundred thousand men strong, in the Emperour Rodolphus his time, and after they were driven out of the countrey, the Emperour built this on their works for a memoriall, the garden is almost foure-square, encircled with a strong stone wall, and at every corner a faire Tower, and in the middle two, with three partitions in everie one, and the tops covered with brasse, round within the wall is a walke for two to goe a brest, covered with brasse, and underset thicke with pillars of stone: then returned wee to another very stately large garden of the Empresses neere unto the citie, called her Favorita, having severall small gardens adjoyning to it and a faire house: the next day his Excellence went to see the Queene againe, and the two Princes her Sonne and Daughter here we staid a weeke, and departed the first of Iuly by waggons for Prague, passing first over three long bridges handing over severall branches of the Danubius: so by the wals of Cornyburgh the towne aforementioned, to Stackay a poore village where wee dined, after dinner by Kildersdorf to Holebrum a poore village, where wee lay all night on the straw, having travelled seven Dutch miles, and every Dutch mile is foure English, where six and twentie houses were burnt that day fortnight wee came, by thunder and

<25>

40

lightning, the next day early from hence passing thorow plaines and corne-fields which were a reaping, we came to Kudordorp, where Moravia begins in a great plaine, where two stones are set in the ground, dividing Lower Austria and Moravia, then past we thorow Colendorp the first towne in Moravia, and by a Crosse standing in a plaine not neere any towne, with many graves about it, then to Swamb a prettie towne where we dined, having past that fore-noone in danger neere a great company of Crabats, who were thereabouts, who frighted the towne: for when his Excellencies Harbenger entred the gates an houre before us, they were all shutting up of their shops, and running out to defend the towne. After dinner thorow most plaines and corne-fields which were a reaping, untill wee came at Bodewich, a poore village, where wee lay on the plancher, and travelled that day seven Dutch miles.

The next day being Sunday, and the third of Iuly, we stayed there untill dinner, and thence thorow part of a wood called Hertz-waldt, on a causey two English miles long, the wood being three hundred miles in length {as we were credibly informed} passing thorow we saw severall fires in it, & many strange things are likewise seene, and so by Bernetz, a little towne at the end of the wood, to Iglo, a beautifull built towne seated on a little hill, where we lay that night, having gone foure Dutch miles and an halfe. Earely the next morning from thence passing over a River at the end of the towne, which parteth Moravia and Bohemia, and then thorow Stickey the first towne in Bohemia, so thorow Haybeireitz a village, in which an Oast killed at severall

<26>

times of his guests ninetie men, and made meat of them, so to Dutchbrade a towne where wee dined, and then departed, passing thorow a plaine wooddie countrey to Holebrum, where we lay that night on the plancher, which was a most fearefull night of thunder and lightning, having travelled seven Dutch miles.

The next morning wee departed, and went thorow a wooddie countrey againe, and thorow a towne called Shasshaw where in the street we passed thorow, lieth buried the body of one Iohn Ziska, who made war against the Emperour Rodolphus, in the defence of his deere friend

Iohn Hus, who died a Martyr: this Iohn Ziska in all his wars was a victor, and when hee was blinde desired to bee carried up and downe the wars, and at his death commanded that a Drum might be made of his skin, which was done, and wheresoever that was, they subdued likewise; then by a silver Mine of the King of Hungaries, which was by the way side on a little hill, into which wee entred to see their works, the oare being two hundred and fiftie fathom deepe, and behinde this place is a citie called Kettenburgh, which wee left two English miles of our left hand and thence to Colen two English miles off likewise where we dined; about part of the towne runs the River Elbe: after dinner we past thorow a plaine countrey to Bemishbrade, where wee lay on the plancher againe, having travelled eight Dutch miles, which hath beene a faire built towne, and very pleasantly seated, but now burnt almost downe by a Carpenter, when the Emperour was in it, and since been pillaged twice, by the Swedish, and the Duke of Bavaria his forces.

<27>

The next morning earely, being the sixth of Iuly, from thence to Prague to dinner, being five Dutch miles, passing first thorow very pleasant plaines and meddowes, vntill we came neere the citie, which is encompassed on both sides with rocks and hils, all planted with vines, having three townes belonging to it, Newstadt, Oldstadt, and the Slostadt; at Newstadt wee entred in at a faire gate, passing thorow into Oldstadt, to his Excellencies lodging, which said Stadt is inhabited chiefly by Iewes, who have there foure Synagogues, and in one I saw there a Rabbi circumcise a child, here we were told that all their fruits in the further parts of the countrey were spoyled, as corne, vineyards, and the like, by the aforesaid thunder and lightning with hailestones as big as ones fist, and also divers cattell were then lost: between this and the Slostadt runneth a pleasant river called the Muldow, and over it standeth a faire Bridge of stone, as long as London Bridge, over which his Excellencie passed, going to view the Castle, being a stately large built Fort, seated on a high hill within the Slostadt, called Ketschin [=Hradschin], in which the King of Bohemia lived first wee passed thorow three faire

Court-yards, having at one of the gates a guard of Souldiers in which Court-yard there is a statue of S. George on
horse-backe in brasse, and a fountaine, then entred we into
a spacious hall, having many faire shops in it like unto
Westminster, but that their Courts of Iudicature are in
other roomes by it: from hence wee went up and passed
thorow many faire roomes well hung, and pictures in
them, and one roome furnished with English pictures of
our Nobilitie, which the King of Bohemia was forced to
leave,

<28>

passing thus untill wee came at one roome two stories
high, which was their Councell-chamber, where the Bo-
hemians being sat at Councell, and three of the Emperours
Councell with them, there rose a mutiny, insomuch that
they threw them three out on the ground, which was fiftie
five foot high, and shot pistols after them, yet none of
them killed, and two of them still alive, and upon that
ground they fell on are set set up three gilt crosses: then
went we downe into a stately lower roome, which used to
bee their masking roome, upholden with severall faire

pillars, in the middle, and statures of brasse placed by them; by the wals hang pictures of Indian horses which were there then; adjoyning to this is a large dining roome, having a table in it of Mozaique worke, and musicke within it not to be discerned, then at the end of this roome is a little place where choyce armour is, and one Piece which I saw shot off a bullet, not having any powder in it: then into the Schant kamber [=Schatzkammer], where the treasure was, and a most noble collection of the Emperour Rodolphus.

In the first roome was cup-boords placed in the wals on our right hand; the first was of corall; the second, of Purslaine; the third, of mother of pearle; the fourth, of curious brasse-plates engraven; the fifth and sixth, Mathematicall Instruments; the seventh, Basons, Ewers, and cups of Amber; the eighth, cups of Aggets, Gold and Chrystall; the ninth of rocks; the tenth, of Mozaique worke in stone; the eleventh, cups of Ivorie, and a great Unicornes horne a yard in length; the twelfth, of imbossing worke; the thirteenth, of Brasse pictures; the foureteenth, of antick

<29>

things cast in silver; the fifteenth, cabinets of Bohemia Diamonds, and little chests of Bohemia pearle; the sixteenth, things belonging to Astronomy; the seventeenth and eighteenth, Indian worke; the nineteenth, Turkey-worke; the twentieth, of a lively statue of a woman covered with taffatie. Then in the middle of the roome are rare clocks of all kinds; the first was like a globe with musike; the second was set round about the middle with little pillars, and a bullet running round in a cresse out and in, and over it hung two little cords, which being puld, wee heard sweet musike, but could not discerne from whence it was; the third had a faire lively face and hand looking out, and musike with voyces singing, not to be discovered; the fourth, a close clocke, and by it a faire table of Mozaique worke; the fifth, with foure ascents set severally with pillars, and a bullet running round in a cresse up to the top, playing with musike; the sixth, like the top of a globe, the gold coloured like a green field, and a Bucke running round in and out, and hounds after making a noyse, and beneath musike, and Anticks, dancing in a round within it; the seventh, a clocke with a globe: by the wals on the other side anticke things set up, and pictures, together with a steele chaire very curiously wrought and cut thorow. Then entred wee into another little closet, wherein were more cabbins placed in the wals on the same side, of presents sent to the Emperour, as gilt helmets and head peeces, and statues.

In the third roome, foure cup-boords in the wals full of rare pictures, and in the middle of the roome anticke things, as a Bore rough cast to the life, and a

<30>

statue of a strong Maid to the life, who went to war, and a presse of ancient bookes. The fourth roome, three cup-boords full of the Anatomies of severall rarities, as Cockatrices, and fishes part resembling men; and the fourth cup-boord of rare great shels; the fifth, of fine dishes; the sixth, of all kinde of little shels, and a Librarie, with one mightie great booke in folio, written by a Fryar in a dungeon, who was there put in, upon some hainous offence there to suffer, and fortie yeeres after discovered by some Fryars going neere, hearing a noyse, had search made, and found him, who brought forth this booke, consisting of the old and new Testament, and many strange histories, which hee was all that time a writing, and assisted by the Devill – as he conceived – and spake very little more before he died.

Here is likewise all the skins of those Indian horses, whose pictures hung up in the masking roome: then did wee enter into a large Church, standing neere about the middle of the Castle, where about the Quire are cut in wood many fine things, and a tombe of the Queenes Confessour, called Iohan[nes] Nepomews, who was miserably tortured by Wenceslaus the fourth King of Bohemia, to reveale her Majesties confession, and at last put to death by him, Anno Dom[ini] 1383, from hence his Excellencie went to view a garden behind the castle within the wall, where wee went in a walke covered arbour-like, halfe an English mile long, untill we came at a stately old building, with walkes round the house, and set thicke with pillars and likewise on the top of the house, with a delightfull prospect over all the citie, and then his Excellencie returned backe to

<31>

the Keepers house, and there dined, having sent provision before: dinner being past, his Excellencie went to see a Parke two English miles off the Citie, in which there is a Friarie of white Friars, who were leaping then in the Parke, as wee passed by to see a great beast called a Buffule, which is kept there, and then returned home by Wallensteines new house, into which his Excellencie entred to view it, first passing thorow a large hall of eight and thirtie paces, or more in length, and one and twentie in breadth, we went up thorow galleries having pictures hung up, and painted on the wals with stories of Hercules, above head divers stories of Ovid; then to the Audience-roome, where the foure elements are in the middle above head, and thorow other faire chambers; then downe into the garden, where there are five fountaines, and great figures of brasse placed on them, and on the great fountaine Neptune, with foure Nymphs about him, and a faire Grott-house, but the waters run not; then into the stable, being curiously built, where six and twentie horses may stand, the pillars and manger all of red marble, and thirtie eight in number, and each pillar cost twentie five pounds, there are foure Court-yards which encompasseth the house, which is now the King of Hungaries.

This Wallensteine was sole Commander of the Empire, under the Emperour, and grew so great, which caused his Majestie to be jealous of him, as he had just cause considering his plots which hee had laid against the Crowne; but to prevent the worst, privately tooke order with some of his Irish Captaines, who were appointed to keepe watch of him that night, to

<32>

cut him off, which was effected in the evening, pressing on the sudden into his chamber found him onely in his shirt, and said, "Live Ferdinando, but dye traytour Wallensteine"; at which he opened his armes and cried, "Oh my God", embracing the stabs of the halberds, which done, they cut off his head, and presently posted to the Emperour with it, who gave them great rewards, and they still continue much in his favour.

The next day his Excellence was invited to a play at the Iesuites College, where the Senior of the house is an Irish man, and there entertained Prince-like; first, an oration by a young Scholler, then passing downe by a Guard of Souldiers, who discharged their muskets: his Excellence being past to the roome where the Comedy was acted, which action did please exceedingly, not onely in respect of substance, but also for the goodnesse of the action and severall habits, in number more than fiftie, the chiefe part were young Schollers, and divers of them Barons sons, and being ended, desired to kisse his Excellencies hand kneeling, in testimony of his approbation. And here is the argument annexed in the page following.

<33>

Pax in Anglia, diu exul in Germaniam postliminio reditura.

Drama,

Cum Illustrissimus & Excellentissimus Thomas Howardus, Arundelliae & Surriae Comes, & Potentissimi Caroli Magnae Britanniae Regis ad Augustissimum Imperatorem Ferdinandum secundum, & Imperii Principes Legatus Extraordinarius, Collegium Societatis Iesu inviserit, a Collegii studiosis datum Pragae, 1636.

Prologus.

Mercurii famulus in theatro apparando occupatus, in parvos pueros incidit Regis Angliae Legatum videre cupidos: negat ex theatro spectari posse nisi adventum ei gratulentur, cum Latine per aetatem tenellam non possint, diverso Idiomate vernaculo id praestent.

Pars prima.

Scena prima.

Mercurius Deos Deasque, proprio quemque comitatu, & schemate, ad concilium venientes excipit, & loca distribuit.

Scena secunda.

Astraea apud Iovem Deosque de mortalium sceleribus queritur. Iupiter auditis sententiis, orbem Marti, Vulcanoque puniendum tradit.

Scena tertia.

Pax desolata quaerit locum ubi Martis furorem declinet, Neptunus in Angliam marina choncha eam vehit.

<34>

Scena quarta.

Mars globum terrae in varias partes dividit, & Bellonae furori caeterisque asseclis distribuit.

Scena prima.

Ceres, Apollo, & Bacchus deplorant apud Iovem, illam quam a Marte patiuntur calamitatem: Iupiter ad Neptunum eos destinat.

Scena secunda.

Neptunus se Carolo Britanniae Regimaris imperium commisisse nunciat, illum adeant pro pace orbi reddenda.

Scena tertia.

Mercurius bene sperare Cererem & Phoebum jubet, Carolum Regem Pacem brevi reducturum per Legatum Howardum Arundelliae Comitem: pristinis sedibus se restituendam Pax asserit: gratulantur sibi omnes, & Howardo applaudunt.

Ad Gentilicia Howardicae Familiae Symbola alludens faelicia omnia Legato & apprecatur & ominatur, & eum veneratus, suo & omnium nomine gratias agit.

Plaudite.

<35>

Peace is in England, which having beene a long while exiled, and given over as gone, is now about to returne into Germany.

A Masque

When the most Illustrious and most Excellent, Thomas Howard Earle of Arundell and Surrey, Extraordinarie Ambassadour from his Puissant Majestie of Great Britaine, to the most August Emperour Ferdinand the Second, and to the rest of the Princes of Germany, came to visit the Iesuites College, presented by the Students at Prague, 1636.

The Prologue.

Mercuries servant imployed about making ready of the Theatre, fals upon little children, who would faine see the Ambassadour of the King of England: he tels them that they cannot see him in the Theatre, unlesse they will congratulate his comming: whom when by reason of their tender age they cannot salute in Latine, they doe performe it in their native language in a differing Idiome.

The first Part.

The first Scene.

Mercury entertaines the Gods and Goddesses with their severall attendants, in a proper habit, comming to Councell, and appoints to every one their places.

<36>

The second Scene.

Astraea complaines to Iupiter and the rest of the Gods of the crimes of men. Iupiter having heard their opinions, delivers over the world to be punished by Mars and Vulcan.

The third Scene.

Peace now forlorne seeks out for a place where she may secure herselfe from the fury of Mars. Neptune carries her over into England in a sea-shell.

The fourth Scene.

Mars divides the globe of the earth into divers parts, and distributes them to the furie of Bellona and his other agents.

The second Part.

The first Scene.

Ceres, Apollo, and Bacchus bewaile before Iupiter the calamitie which they suffer from Mars: Iupiter sends them unto Neptune.

The second Scene.

Neptune tels them that hee hath committed the Imperiall government of the sea to Charles King of Great Britaine, and that they must make suit to him to restore peace unto the world.

The third Scene.

Mercury bids Ceres and Apollo to be of good cheere, and wils them not to doubt, but that King Charles will shortly by his Ambassadour Howard Earle of Arundle, reduce Peace. Peace affirmeth that shee shall be restored

<37>

to her former dwellings, they doe all gratulate one another, and give their acclamations to Howard.

The Epilogue

Alluding to the Armes of the House of the Howards, both wish and presage all happinesse to the Ambassadour, and having made obeysance to him, give him thanks for himselfe, and for all the rest.

[The Journal, to be continued]

Here we stayed seven dayes, and departed the thirteenth of Iuly for Regenspurg by waggons, over the plaine
where the great battell was fought, betweene the Emperour and the King of Bohemia, not above two English miles
from the citie, there wee did observe many places in the
ground, wherein the dead bodies were put, and a great
company of bones lying by on a heape, where were slaine
in all on both sides about thirtie thousand: from thence
thorow a plaine corne countrey, to a little towne three
Dutch miles from Frague, called Beroum, where wee lay,
which towne hath beene burnt by the Duke of Saxon his
forces. The next morning earely wee went thorow plaine
corne-fields and meddowes, untill we came to Mauth, a
poore village where we dined: from thence thorow woods,
and by poore villages burnt, to a prettie towne called Pilsen, where we lay that night, having travelled seven Dutch
miles, it is seated in a plaine,

<38>

with three little rivers running by it, as Misen, Glatow,
and Pilsen, taking the name from the towne.

The next morning thorow a wooddie countrey and corne-fields to Swabe to dinner; after dinner to Bishop-steine to bed, having this day travelled but foure Dutch miles, in which the Count Dorfmastaff hath a little castle pleasantly seated, and the river Igree running about part of it, the towne was never pillaged as yet. Earely the next morning from thence passing thorow a very stony hill, and a wood foure English miles in length, called Bemer-waldt [=Böhmerwald], wherein about the middest there is a Schans, in which Count Mansfelt and his Armie lay two moneths, at which Schans the upper Palatinate begins. Then to Waldminiken, a little towne to dinner, the first in the upper Palatinate; and the Oast of the house did serve Count Mansfelt as Ancient at that time: after dinner thorow a wooddie poore countrey to Redtz a little towne where we lay that night, having travelled six Dutch miles.

The seventeenth day being Sunday, early we departed, passing thorow great woods, in danger of the Crabats lying thereabouts, and carried out of our way by (by) chance through an ignorant guide, untill we came to Bruke, a towne miserably ruinated, seated pleasantly in a plaine, where there was not above foure poore housholds remaining: not long since it was in great prosperitie; for when wee were a little past the towne, there was a gallowes and scaffold by the way, whereon the Burgers of the towne suffered, and many hanging still, who were Lutherans: then to a towne called Nettenow to dinner, and from thence after dinner to Regenspurg, having travelled seven

<39>

Dutch miles this day, passing first thorow many pleasant places of landskips, and over the river Regen, which runneth into the Danuby just by the citi, passing over on rafters, the bridge being beaten downe then with the other former batteries: between Vienna and this place, are many faire built townes promising much, by reason of their severall Piazzo's, or Market-places and Fountaines, with other such expressions, but entring the houses, scarse finde men, lodging, or people of understanding to exchange discourse with. The next day after his Excellence came hither, the Ambassadour of the Elector of Brandenburg visited him; and the day after his Excellence visited him againe; here his Excellence stayed but foure dayes, because the

Emperour was not come, and departed for Augusta, on Thursday the one and twentieth of Iuly, and dined that day at Sall, a small towne on the Danuby, thence thorow Bavaria to Augsburg, a verie fine towne standing on the river Volga, which a little before fals into the Danuby, and thence that night to Neistadt, a faire towne ten miles from Regenspurg, where his Excellence lay that night.

Next day earely passing thorow a fine wooddie countrey to Bezanzon, where my Lady Abbesse gave his Excellence a banquet, from thence after dinner to Palermo, a stately towne, and there lay that night, having travelled seven Dutch miles. Satturday being the three and twentieth of Iuly, we departed for Augusta, passing thorow part of Tiroll to Mumantia, burnt some two yeeres since by Generall Cleandor, one of the King of Swedens Colonels; and from thence to Dole, which hath been a verie pleasant situated towne, standing

<40>

on the brow of a hill, from whence at the distance of three English miles we beheld Augusta, which towne of Dole was also with Bezanzow burnt by Colonell Cleandor two yeeres since, passing thorow this towne, we descended into a goodly valley, but [th]ere we gat into it, went over a small arme of the river Tanais, {which encompasseth Augusta on the West, as the river Vindilicorum doth on the East} passing this valley, which is the more famous, in respect at the upper end of it was fought the great battell of Pharsalia, between Pompey & Iulius Caesar, from whence it takes the name of the Plaine of Pharsalia: drawing neere Augusta, we passed over five bridges standing over the river Vindilicorum, which is divided into so many branches so running with so many Bulwarks: the river water is of an excellent greene colour, which is caused – as they say – running out of Copperas mines, which are in the mountaines of Dalmatia, from whence it springs, taking its name from Vindix a famous Captaine, who first rebelled against Nero, passing over all these bridges, we entred the outer towne, which is well built, and so in at a broad port thorow the high street to his Excellences lodging, that day and the next was spent in seeing pictures: Munday being the five and twentieth day, his Excellence went to see the Stadt-house. First you must understand it to bee a square pile, of at least one hundred foot square; in the middest against the street, yee enter by a large paire of staires of thirteene steps, into a stately lower roome supported by twelve Calcidonian pillars, opposite to which against the wals stand the images of the first Caesars, which because they were written under,

<41>

I will mention as first, Augustus the City Founder, from whence it takes the name, then Tiberius, Nero, Sergius, Andronicus, Meleager, Themistocles, Lysimachus, Orion, Phoebus, Enobarbus, and Barbarossa, over it in another roome which to come to, wee passed up sixe and thirty staires which as the other was supported by twelve Pillars of Corinthian worke and Jasper stone, in which is painted to the life {which they say, was done by Apelles and Michael Angelo, the one the master the other the man} are the Images of Lycurgus, Zeno, Aristocrates, Aristides, Agathocles, Phocion, Anaxagoras, the first Triumvirat of Rome, thence by thirty steppes more into the State-house it selfe, which is a most curious peece of Worke, without Pillers, peeced with Onyx and Smarage, two excellent kindes of Marble, found in the Teneriffe a mountaine of Tiroll, it is about the Walles painted with the Stories of all the gods, painted by Raphael Urbine, some twelve yeeres since, against this State-house stands a goodly Fountaine in the middle on a Pedastall of Brasse, the Statue of Augustus environed with all the gods and goddesses to the number of forty in Brasse in Polonian Cassockes and Turkish Scymiters by their sides, in the middest of the high street is another of Mercurie, and at the farther end Hercules in a Lions skinne killing of Hydra with his seventy heads all in Brasse, which as soone as he strikes off one head, two ariseth in the place, there are besides in this Towne many other rare things, as an Arsenall brave

\<42\>

Monasteries Fugger house, water workes most innumerable and admirable rare and curious buildings and what not to delight the eye, heere his Excellency staied a weeke. And thence on Sunday, hearing the Emperour was a comming to Regenspurg, departed that day being the one and thirty of Iuly another way for Regenspurg through the Mountaines of Tiroll to Niburg, where wee lay being seven Dutch miles, a stately Towne from whence the Duke of Niburg takes his name, it stands on a small River Boristines which is of a blacke colour, as rising out from the cole Mines of Epirus.

The next day through Swaben and to Ingolstate the strongest Towne in all Mesia, which is a part of Bavaria, which Towne kept out the King of Sweden and killed his Horse under him, whose skinne is preserved still for a Relique in the Arsenall, it is the stronger having the Danu and a large Plaine on the South, and the swift River Rhodanus on the North, which not above a mile before falles into the Danu.

The next day which was the third of August his Excellency tooke Boate and that night arrived at Regenspurg, passing first by many small places not worth the naming except Rellein, a great Towne which had anciently beene a Colony De Corvinus, the Dictators, as it is said. The Emperours comming to Towne was in this manner: when he entered the first Gate of the City, twelve of the Magistrates, standing there, made a long Oration

<43>

to his Majesty after their duty done, then past through a round where Musicke and voyces were, and a Canopie borne by sixe men having his Majesties Armes thereon, passing thus along the Streets through seven hundred Souldiers placed in order and his owne Guard of an hundred men about his Coach, the Empresse being with him, and after his Coach were an hundred Horsemen, with Carabines and Pistols, who always guard his Person, called Harshers, clothed alike, then followed the Archdutchesse, in her Coach, and all the rest in their degrees, untill they came at the great Church, where his Majesty alighted and went in, where the Bishoppe of the City met him at the enterance, being clothed in his robes, with his Miter Cope and Croysers Staffe, burnt incense to them, being upon their knees, after went up to the high Altar, and there heard Te Deum sung with Drummes and Trumpets, this ended, retyred into his Pallas which doth adjoyne to the Church.

The fifth day his Excellency had audience of the Emperour and Emperesse, the next day Conde d'Oniato the

Spanish Ambassadour Extraordinary visited his Excellency guarded by twelve Polakes having Carabines on their shoulders and sables by their sides, whose sonne is now Ambassadour Extraordinary in England.

The nineth day his Excellencie visited him, the same day the Duke of Bavaria came, and his Dutchesse, being bigge with childe, was brought

<44>

in her chaire from the waters side, attended with eight hundred thirty and seven persons, and seven hundred sixty and foure horses, and have taken five hundred quarters for them heere in the Towne.

The next day being Sunday, the Bishop of Mentz came in the evening with an hundred seventy and nine horses, and one hundred eighty and five persons.

The sixteenth day the Poland Ambassadour visited his Excellency having thirty followers being all clothed in severall coloured Sattin dublets and red cloth hose with long Poland red coates, most of woven silke, without sleeves bands or hats, but redde cappes on their heads with a feather like unto a Turkey's in every one of them, their haire all cut off their heads, but one long locke left on their crowne, and all yellow short bootes, no spurres but iron heeles, and the Ambassadour in the same fashion, and twelve footemen clothed in the same kinde in a meaner habit, having great Pole-axes in their hands and sables by their sides.

The eighteenth day being the Emperours Coronation day[5], his Majestie went to visite the Elector of Mentz, about eight of the clocke in the morning, and all his Nobles and Servants attending on his Person going before him afoote by two and two together.

The same day also as soone as his Majesty departed, his Excellency visited him: and the one and

<45>

twenty being Sunday the Venetian Ambassadour visited his Excellency, and after him the Florentine Agent.

The next day in the afternoone his Excellency was visited by the Elector of Mentz, and the Bishop of Vienna after him, and Marquis Palavicino.

---

[5] Ferdinand III., Körnung zum König 1636.

The five and twenty day in the forenoone the Holland Ambassadour visited his Excellency.

And the next day the Spanish Ambassadour gave his Excellency the second visite, and after him the Count Slavata Chancellour of Prague.

The eight and twenty day being Sunday in the forenoone, the Emperour and Empresse went to doe homage for peace, accompanied with the Bishop of Mentz, the Duke of Bavaria, his Dutchesse, and the Archduchesse her sister, from his Palace to a little old Church in the Towne, going all a foote, and their Nobles and servants attending in their orders; first Bannors, then all the Cavaleers, then singers, and all the Priests with their Orders, and the Bishop of the Towne in his Church Robes, then the Emperour following, led by the Count Kezell Lord high Chamberlaine, and Don-Baltazar, a great Commander: the Emperesse led by Count Slavata and Prince Dietreichstain, Lord high Chamberlaine to her Majestie; the Bishop of Mentz, the Duke of Bavaria, his Dutchesse, and the Archdutchesse her sister, led by their servants, and all the Nobles and Ladies following in their degrees: after their devotions ended, returned in the same manner.

<46>

The same day in the afternoone, his Excellency visited the Spanish Ambassadour.

And the next day the Bishop of Maintz gave his Excellencie the second visite.

This day after great search, were found the lost Bodies of his Excellencies servants, the Gentleman of his horse, his Trumpeter, together with their Guide, the Postmaster: sixe daies after the murder committed, being most barbarouslie slaine and tied to severall trees in the Wood, the distance of about a Pistols shot off from the Highway, as it was conceived to bee spectators each one of anothers end, and not foure English miles from Nuringburge, taken as they were returning for Regenspurge, and thus murthered: the head of the Gentleman of the Horse shotte thorough with a Pistoll, the Trumpeters head cut off, and the Guides cloven in sunder, and the next day after they were found were nobly interred at Nuringburge, accompanied with all the Lords and Burgers of the Citie.

The first of September [01.09.163x] being Thursday in the morning, came the Bishoppe of Vienna and Doctor Gebard, one of the Emperors Counsell, and a Clarke of the Counsell, to conferre together about his Excellencies Ambassage.

The fourth day being Sunday, the Emperour, Emperesse, the Dutchesse of Bavaria, and the Archduchesse her sister, went to the holy Crosse to heare a Vesper sung, and the Nobles afoote by their Coaches; the next day about ten

<47>

of the clocke in the forenoone all the Electors or their Ambassadours mette privately at Court, the same day, the Countesse of Tyrconnell an Irish Lady, and Sir Griffin Markham an English Gentleman dined with his Excellency, and many Scotish and Irish Colonels hath visited his Excellencie and dined with him likewise; and they say a great part of the Emperours Army bee our Kings Subiects.

The next day the Spanish Ambassadour gave his Excellency the second visit, and after him, the Leger of Genoa.

71

The eighth day being Thursday, about eight of the clocke in the morning, all the Electors or their Ambassadours met in the State-house, being a little meane house where the Magistrates of the Towne sit to doe Justice, comming in this manner; first the Elector of Collen his Ambassadour, the Elector of Brandeburgh his Ambassadour, Elector of Mentz, the Duke of Bavaria, and the Elector of Saxon his Ambassadour, but the Elector of Tryer who was taken prisoner by the Spaniard as afore mentioned was not admitted, all in their Coaches, having but few attendants, and fewer spectators, they being sat, two chaines were drawne over the Street and guarded that none might passe neere, having sat two howers departed in the same manner they came, the Elector of Mentz, is Chancellour of Germanie, the Elector of Collen Chancellour of Italy, the King of Bohemia Cup-bearer of the Empire, the Elector Palatine of the Rhine

<48>

high Shewer of Germanie, the Elector of Saxon high Marshall of the Empire, and the Elector of Brandeburg

72

high Chamberlaine of the Empire: this day the Emperours propositions were opened and read to them.

His first was, that they should depose Tryer from his Electorship, and elect Leopaldus his Majesties second sonne in his place.

The second, to crowne his sonne King of the Romanes, who is now King of Hungary.

The third to raise up Forces to cleare the Empire of all Enemies which detaine and keepe any Imperiall Townes.

The fourth, to conclude a generall peace with all Christian Princes.

The tenth day, they all sat againe, and in a meaner fashion than before.

The fifteenth day, sat againe, in the forenoone there was a man beheaded for committing incest with his owne daughter, from nine yeeres old untill this time, she being now of the age of twelve yeeres, and with childe by him.

In the afternoone about foure of the clocke, came the Poland Ambassadour, to visit his Excellency, being his second time.

The next day in the morning earely, the Duke of Bavaria and his Dutchesse departed for Munecken eighteene Dutch miles off, there to remaine untill shee bee delivered; in so meane a fashion not worthy so much as to bee named, onely

<49>

shee was caried in a Chaire by her Coaches side.

The two and twentieth day, the Electors sate againe, and the most part of the day[6] they spent by way of private visits, with one another.

The next day, the Brandenburgs Ambassador, gave his Excellence the second visite.

The foure and twentieth day, the Ambassador of Holland visited his Excellence againe.

October the fourth day, the Count Megaw visited his Excellence the second time.

The fift[h] day [=05.10.1636 jul. / 15.10.1636 greg.] in the morning, the Emperour, Empresse, and all the Court, went to the Church of the Carmelites, to celebrate the Feast of St. Tereza, by whose Prayers and intercessions, it

---

[6] In der Vorlage „Dyet".

is sayd, certaine Captives were delivered out of Turkie, transported out of their bondage and set free, in another place not farre distant, and their Irons, Fetters, and Pictures, still preserved in this Church, for a testimony of the myracle: In the afternoone, the King of Hungary came, being sent for by the Emperor from the Army, to be elected King of the Romans, accompanied with divers Colonels and Commanders of Scotch and Irish, but an English Mile off the Town his Majesty made a stay, being in his Coach, untill the Emperor, Empresse and the whole Court came forth to meet him, and then he and all his Followers tooke horse, and met the Emperour and Empresse at a distance, he lighted, and hastened to doe his obedience to them; they likewise embracing him, then returned to his sister the Archdutchesse to salute her, who was in another Coach; in the meane time, his Followers kist the Emperor and Empresse hands; that ended, the

<50>

Emperor call'd him into his Coach, and went a Hawking, but when they came at the place where their game was, they all tooke Horse, but the Empresse and the

Archdutchesse, who were carryed in an open Litter by Mules, their sport being ended, returned with their three Spaniels and one Hawke to their Pallace.

The 7. day, his Excellence was visited by Colonell Lesley a Scotch Commander, and Captaine of the King of Hungaries Guard.

The 10. day on Sunday, the King went poste to meet with his Queene, who was a comming hither likewise.

The 12. day, the Elector of Colen came in the forenoone, very well attended, and in the evening his Excellence had audience of the Emperor and Empresse, but as we passed through the Chambers to her Majesty, there were neyther lights, nor men to direct us the way, passing thus along in the darke untill wee stumbled on a little doore, which is the doore of their Antichamber, where wee found three or foure Cavalieres, who had runne from the Emperours side thither a little before, to informe her Majesty of his Excellence's comming, who was instantly brought in to her Chamber, and after returned the same way, and but one attending with a light.

The fourteenth day being Friday, the Queene of Hungarie came about five of the clocke in the afternoone, for at one, the Emperour, Empresse, and the Elector of Collen, together with the whole Court, went three English miles from the Towne to meet her, but Hawked as hee went untill three a clock, and then

<51>

discovering her a comming about halfe an English mile distant, left his sport and went to meet her, drawing neere, lighted of his Horse about foure Rod off from her Coach, and made hast with his Hat in hand to imbrace her, shee being but got out of her Coach and comming a little towards him, did her obedience kneeling and kissed his Hand, hee bowing low likewise, most joyfully received her in his armes, the Empresse being in a Litter and the Archdutchesse, hastened out likewise to salute her; their gratulation being ended, betweene them and the Elector of Collen and Conde d'Oniato, the Spanish Ambassador extraordinary, which in all, held more than a quarter of an houre, the King and Queene returned home in the

Emperours Coach, having about thirty Coaches, and one hundred Horse, which brought them into the Towne.

The 17. day at 9 of the clocke in the morning, his Excellence had audience of the King, and in the afternoone was visited by Colonell Lesley againe, and after him by the Agent of Poland.

The next day in the Evening, there was a great Marriage at Court, Colonell Wager a Polander, who married a Maid of honour to the Empresse, call'd Madam Shafcutzin, whose Father was beheaded some few yeares since here in this Towne as a Conspirator against the Emperor; the Ceremony of the marriage beeing contrary to our English fashion, and in the Evening: I will declare it; First hee beeing brought from his Lodging by the Poland Ambassadour and many Cavalieres all well mounted

<52>

to the Court, lighted and went up to the Emperour and Empresse, then to his Majesties private Chappell, being brought thither by the Emperor & the King, and she by the Empresse and the Queen, where the Bishop onely joyned their hands, as the Emperor gave her, and set a rich

Crowne of Diamonds and Pearle on his head, which was his Majesties, and then returned to the Privie Chamber, where the Emperor gave them a Supper, and his Majesty, the Empresse, the King and Queene of Hungary, and the Archdutchesse, together with the Elector of Mentz and Colen, sate at Table with them, and the Bridegroome with the Crowne all the time on, and the Bride cloathed very richly at the Empresses charge, having no other Iewels on but her Majesties that night, and after Supper put to Bed by them, being an order, that what Lady soever of the Court Marries they do lye there that night, if she be a Maide, not else.

The next day at two of the clocke, Count Trausmistorfe Privie Councellor to the Emperor, and the chiefe Ruler in all the King of Hungaries affaires, visited his Excellence, being sent from the King.

The day after, Colonell Lesley dined with his Excellence, and after dinner was visited by the Spanish Ambassador Conde d'Oniato.

And the one and twentieth day, his Excellence had Audience of the King and Queene of Hungarie, at Two of the clocke in the afternoone.

The next day, his Excellence visited Count Trausmistorfe, and the Bishop of Vienna, and then returned home, and presently after Count Schlyck President to

<53>

the Councell of warre, visited his Excellence; and at five of the clocke came Marquis Castillado to Towne, being Ambassador in ordinary from Spaine, who alwayes accompanies the King of Hungary in the Army, and came now from thence.

The 23. being Sunday, the Count of Schwartzenburg his Sonne, whose Father is the Ambassador from the Prince of Brandenburg, and Colonell Lesley, dined with his Excellence.

And the foure and twentieth day, about eight of the clocke in the morning, his Excellence visited the Elector of Colen, and at two of the clock Marquis Castillado, and likewise the Count Megaw.

And the day following, hee visited the Poland Ambassador in the forenoone, and the Elector of Mentz in the afternoone.

The 26. day, young Pappenheym dyned with his Excellence, whose Father was Generall for the Emperour in the King of Swedens time, and slaine then.

And the next day, his Excellence visited the Count of Schlyck againe.

The 28. his Excellence visited the Count of Trausmistorfe: Being returned home, the Poland Ambassador came to take his leave of his Excellence, and returned into Poland againe; and this day the Elector of Tryer past by the Town at a distance, going for Lintz, there to remaine a Prisoner during the Emperours pleasure, being brought out of the King of Spaines dominions by a Convoy of the Emperors.

The 29. day in the evening, the Elector of Colen
<54>
visited his Excellence: And since, the Dutchesse of Bavaria is brought to Bed of a Sonne, and he Christened by

the name of Ferdinandus Maria Franciscus Ignatius Wolfgangus.

The 30. of October on Sunday, their dyned with his Excellence the Count of Styrenburg, the Count of Schmurbenburg junior, Baron Lambert, and Count Piccolomini, whose Father is Generall of the Emperors Army, which joynes now with the Cardinall-Infant against the French. And after dinner, the Spanish Ambassador Castillado visited his Excellence; and the next day his Excellence visited the Spanish Ambassador extraordinary.

The first of November, his Excellence visited the Count of Schlyck in the Fore-noone, and had audience of the King in the afternoone.

The next day, his Excellence tooke his leave of Castillado the Spanish Liedger, and the Ambassador of Brandenburg.

And the day after, Doctor Vmmius Liedger from the Count of Oldenburg, visited his Excellence; and Colonell Henderson a Scotch Gentleman, & dyned both with him: and after dinner, his Excellence tooke his leave of Count Pappenheym Marshall of the Empire under the Elector of

Saxon, and Count Bockhaym Master of the Horse to the King of Hungary; and the next morning, of the Count of Schlyck, and the Count of Strolensdorfe, Vice-Chancellor of the Empire; and in the afternoone of Count Slavato; and then returned home, and presently came Conde d'Oniato the Spanish Ambassador extraordinary, to give his Excellence his last visit;

<55>

he being gone, his Excellence went and tooke his leave of the Elector of Mentz, and in the evening of the Elector of Colen.

The next day, the Count of Slavato came to give his Excellence his last visit, and after him the Bishop of Vienna: And the next morning Marquis Pallavicino, and after dinner the Ambassador Castillado and the Count Trausmistorfe, and at 5 of the clocke his Excellence took his leave of the Emperor, Empresse, and the King and Queene of Hungary.

And the next morning being Tuesday, the 8. of November, early left Regenspurg returning backe for England the same way to Hemmaw, the first night 3 Dutch miles.

The next day wee travailed five Dutch miles to Nye-marke.

And the third day to Nuremburg, which was five Dutch miles more, where the next morning the Lords of the City came and presented their service to his Excellence, in a long Dutch complement, and after dined with him.

And the next day in the afternoone they came againe, with a present of 40 Flaggons of wine, and three killors of Fish, which was brought in by thirty men all in red Coats, guarded on the armes, with white and red Caps, and then desired his Excellence to goe and view their Stathouse, which is a large long building of Stone, above an hundred paces in length, passing first up 5 ascents of Staires, & through a long Gallery 90 paces long, ruffe cast with sev-erall stories, and at the end entered into a square chamber, which

<56>

sometimes is their Councell-chamber, so into the sec-ond, third and fourth roome, which is twenty eight paces long, and twelve in breadth, painted above head, and carved very richly; and on one of the Walls hang the

Pictures of the sixe Caesars; First, Carolus Magnus, Rodolphus Primus, C[ai]us Mundus[?], Rodolphus Secundus, Mathius Primus, and Ferdinandus this Emperor; then into the fifth roome, which was furnished likewise with severall rare pictures, and two Pictures of Albert Durer and his Father, done by him, which they presented his Excellence with; and in all these roomes are Stoves very richly made, and upholden, some by Lyons of Brasse, and others by Griffons.

From hence, we went to view one of their Houses, in which amongst the rest of his Pictures, was the picture of his Grandfather, who had neyther nose nor chin; as the picture demonstrateth; and then presented his Excellence with a Banquet: from hence to another faire house adjacent, and very well furnished likewise, but before we came into the rooms, we went up the curiousest Stayre-case of stone as ever I have seene.

And from hence to the Castle, where the Father of one of the Lords lived, who after he had shewed his Excellence all the roomes in the Castle, which adjoynes to the wall of the Towne, standing on a Hill, and a very deepe Well of one hundred and fifty Fathom, cut out of a Rocke, by which they were constrayned to releeve the Towne, in the time of their former warres, betweene the Emperor, and the King of Sweden:

<57>

he presented his Excellence with another banquet, and then returned home.

The next day, which was Sunday, they all dined with his Excellence.

And in the morning being the 14. day, wee departed having stayed heere three dayes, and tooke a Convoy of 100 Musketiers along with us to Neustadt, five Dutch miles; The first night, travelling part by Torch-light through the Woods, and there lay on the straw that night: which Towne formerly hath beene inhabited by 250 Burgers or more, and not having now five in it.

The fifteenth day earely, thence to Ketzen five miles, and there lay on the planchers likewise; and the next day to Wirtzburg to dinner, which was three Dutch miles, staying that night there, having no other Towne neere to goe to. After dinner, the Lords of the Towne sent his

Excellence a present of Two and thirty Flaggons of Wine, Fish, and provision for his Horse.

The next morning before his Excellence departed, he was visited by the Bishop of Wesburg, whom wee found, in the habit of a Countrey Gentleman, setting aside his Order, which is an enamelled Crosse hanging on a Blacke ribbon about his necke; who made very much of his Excellence, and presented him with the Picture of our Ladie, done by Albertus Durerus, being one of his best peeces; and then tooke leave of him, who was ready to ride out of Towne, to some other place for safety, the Swedes being within two dayes march of it, and then his Excellence returned

<58>

to his Lodging, and presently went away.

The seaventeenth day, taking a fresh Convoy went to Bishopsheim that night, a Towne seated in a bottome, and incompassed round with Hills, having the River Tauber running about part of it, belonging to the Bishop of Mentz; travelling this day foure Dutch miles and most part through great Woods.

Earely next morning, thence through Kulsen a Village, and divers other poore Villages burnt and pillaged, passing through a hilly wooddy Countrey in much danger of the Croats, and spying some running up and downe in the Woods, being round about us, in number 6.000 or more, dispersing themselves into severall Companies, pillaging and robbing of the Countrey; travelling this day five miles to Mildebarke, but a Dutch mile before wee came thither, entered into our old way at Nunkirken, the poore burnt Village before mentioned, which is now inhabited by some Foure or five poore people.

The 19. day in the morning, from thence another way, taking another fresh Convoy, leaving our old way and the Maine on our right hand, passing along by the side of it, through Hybach a Village, and a faire House which is the Bishop of Mentz likewise, and through other Villages miserably battered, and in Plaines some six English miles in length, untill wee came to Selgenstadt, having gone this day sixe Dutch miles. Falling into our old way within one mile of the Towne, travelling all those dayes in danger of the Croats, where as soone as his Excellence lighted, the Grave Vandosme Governour of the Countrey for

<59>

the Bishop of Mentz, sent his Excellence a present of halfe a wilde Bore, and likewise provision for his Horse; knowing that the Towne could not affoord any thing.

The twentieth day being Sunday, early in the morning, wee went thence to Frankfort to dinner, which was three Dutch miles.

And the next morning after, his Excellence went to Hannaw to visite Sir Iames Ramsey, a Scotch Gentleman and Governour of the Towne, and there stayed that night, who met his Excellence without the gate with a troupe of Horse, and entering the Towne there went off a brace of Canons, and when his Excellence lighted, went off two more by the doore of his Excellencies lodging; which Towne, was besiedged a Yeare and a halfe by the Emperours forces, and at the beginning of the Siege had such a grievous Plague, that there dyed in 7 Weekes, 22.000. yet for all this, they kept out the enemy, though in great want and misery, and three months since it was releeved by the

Landt-grave of Hesse, who slew a great company of the Imperialists and drave the rest away; for as wee passed by afore at a distance, we heard them as they were in their skirmish. The next morning, his Excellence went about the Towne to view the Workes, which are very strong, scarce to bee scaled by any force, having two Engines made but of six Musket barrels a piece, which Dutch Engine dischargeth 80 times together, giving fire to it but once; the Towne is seated in a plaine ground, having the Mayne on the East, and incompassed on the North and West, with the River Knitszig,

<60>

besides Moted round, and this River serveth 14 Mills which adjoynes to the Towne, and before any man can enter into the old Towne he must passe over three Bridges, and through severall Bulworkes, and over another into the new Towne; and at the releefe of the Town, there was one Daniel Lauter a chiefe Burger, dyed for very joy; he being above in his house and seeing the victory, was overcome with such a mighty passion of joy, that hee fell downe and dyed instantly; there was likewise a woman, who killed many Dogs & sold their flesh at a great rate to many people, and one day as shee walked in the Streets, was like to have been devoured by them, had not some poore Souldiers by chance releeved her, who presently confessed what shee had done formerly, acknowledging she had justly deserved it; and after dinner his Excellence tooke leave of Sir Iames Ramsey, and then returned backe to Frankfort.

The foure and twentieth day, foure of the Burgers of the Citie came and presented their service to his Excellence with twenty flaggons of Wine, and then dined with him; here wee stayed three dayes untill our Boates were made ready.

And on Saturday the 26. day of November, wee departed from hence, and rowed downe the Mayne; the first night to Flersheym, which was three miles, against which wee cast anchor and lay aboard; The next morning launched forth, and past downe to Mentz, and there his Excellence went on shore, to see if it were any way inriched since our being there, but alas, wee found it as miserable as before, with divers

<61>

poore people lying on Dunghils almost starved, being scarce able to crawle for to receive his Excellencies almes, and presently returning to our Boate to dinner, wee afterwards releeved many poore hungry soules with the fragments; Thence after dinner downe the Rhyne to Rudeshem, which was five Dutch miles, and there cast anchor, and lay on the boards likewise.

Very earely the next morning wee weyed anchor, and presently entred into a dangerous place to passe, called Bingham-Locke [=Binger Loch], where the River Loo [=Lahn] falls into the Rhyne by the Towne amongst many Rockes, which causeth a violent fall, tossing us up and downe, that if wee had but touched any part of them we had all been cast away; being past this, we came to Bacharach, where, some of our Company did but goe ashore – and presently hastened after in a little Boate, were pursued by five Musketiers almost to his Excellencies Boat, who discharged very often at them, yet by good fortune mist them, and having overtaken his Excellence, they instantly fled away; then going on to a large Iland an English mile from Coblentz, wee there cast anchor and lay all that night; for wee could not passe to the Towne without leave from the Governour, by reason of severall watches which lay in our way; which night wee lay in much danger, perceiving them walke up and downe to catch a prey, for as some of our company did but goe a little way from our Boat, they were layd hold on, and one that fled, had a Musket shot at him, and hee that was taken, they caried before their Commander, who was in a Monastery in the Iland, examining him, & then let him goe.

<62>

The next morning, his Excellence sent againe to the Governour, for passage, who like a base fellow made us stay that night also, and the next day untill three of the clock in the afternoone, and would not let us passe, for all that his Excellence had sent him the Emperors Passe and Letter, wherein hee was commanded, not onely to give passage, but, to assist him in any thing hee required; yet for all this, hee kept us still, and would not give way that our Trumpeter might goe to the French in the Castle; but they perceiving how unworthily hee did deale with his Excellence, discharged 4 or 5 Cannons at his house, and shot quite through it, at last hee came at the third sending for, with an excuse, hee was very unkindly delt with by Cardinall Genetta, the Popes Nuntio, who lately passed by, going to Collen, but stayed him three dayes first, before hee let him passe, and made him promise faithfully not to visit the French, but being got beyond the Towne landed and went in, which made him vow not to let any passe. But after that hee had talked a while with his Excellence, gave leave to fall downe neere the Towne, and having cast anchor, set a strong watch about us, and then gave leave for the Trumpeter to goe to Monsieur Salade in the Castle for passage, who most willingly granted it, and sent his Excellence a very faire ancient Picture; but hearing by the Trumpeter the Governours base usage towards his Excellencie, presently plac'd their Canons against his house, and vowed his Sonne should give fire to them the next morning, and would send him such a breakfast, as that hee should need no dinner; in the

<63>

interim, there came a Lieutenant from the Governour, upon a colour to visite his Excellence, who proved a second

Villaine in the end, for all that wee used him very well, and fedde his hungry belly better than it had beene long before; for the Souldiers themselves confessed, that they had but one Browne loafe and a halfe of Bread in eight dayes, and not one penny of money; yet this Rascall lay lurking in our Boate till our Trumpeter returned, and then violently tooke him and the Skipper, and carried them into the Towne and set a watch about them; and the next morning, sent his Excellence word hee might passe, but the Trumpeter should follow after; whereupon his Excellence sent his Steward to know the reason, who found them tyed by the Armes together, the Skippers finger cut off, & the Trumpeters head escaped very narrowly from being cloven in two, had not his strong Hat defended it, and also had threatned to hang them up the next day together, but with much adoe hee brought them away with him, and after followed a Gentleman to excuse that barbarous base usage of the Lieutenant, and leave to passe, presently departing, and being gone but a little past the Towne and against the Castle, they saluted us, and said they would drinke the King of Englands health, and then gave fire to more than twenty thundring Cannons, beside a brave volley of small Shot, which made their Houses to smoake and tumble in our sight, but they durst not returne one backe againe; the other Governour Geats, gave us very noble usage, but this who was lately sent, shewed himselfe so base, that he deserves

<64>

no name with us; from hence to Bonn, and there cast anchor, but durst not lye nigh the Towne, the Sicknesse being very sore in it, and this day rowed eight miles.

The next day being the first of December, in the morning we went from thence to Collen, being foure miles, leaving those delightfull Mountaines, Hills, and pleasant Vines, and entred into a plaine Countrey, where as soone as wee came into the Towne, neere the Palace where the Cardinall lay, had information, of all what the boorish Governour of Coblentz sayd of him was false; wee stayed heere three dayes untill wee had exchanged our Boates for bigger, and every day his Excellence had presented unto him 24 Flaggons of Wine, sent from the Magistrates; who once dined with him.

And on Sunday the 4. day of December, about foure of the clocke at night tooke Shipping, and the next morning at three a clocke set sayle, and sayled downe by Mulheim on the left side of the Rhyne, and Sonts [=Zons] on the other side, which belongeth to the Abbots of Collen, where wee stayed to free Toll; then on by Newse on the same side, where the River runneth out to it, and so to Dusseldorpe, where as soone as we came but neere the shore, out came the Noble Duke of Neuburgh, and clambered over other Ships to come into ours, to visite his Excellence, being much joyed at his safe returne, and had made provision at his House to entertaine his Excellence, but perceiving he would not stay, sent for a wilde Bore, Wine, and five Pictures, and presented them to his Excellence, then

<65>

tooke his leave, being very sory to let him goe, but considering the time and tediousnesse of the weather, was more willing to give leave, he staying by the shore untill wee put off, and then went off 10 Cannons, the Duke still walking along the shore as farre as the water would give him leave, and stayed untill we were out of sight. From thence by Keiserswert belonging to the Elector of Collen, seated on the left side of the Rhyne, where wee were stayed to free our Toll againe, and at our lanching forth saluted us with one Peece of Ordnance, so on by Ordingen a little Towne, where on the other side, about a league further wee cast anchor, against a small old Castle called Engersort, sayling seaven leagues and a halfe this day, for before wee went by miles, which were some foure or five English miles at the least in length, but these are but three English; this night wee lay in much danger, for there did lye on each side of us, parties, which robbeth and pillageth all Passengers; for wee saw above fifty in a company, going all along by the shore, but a little before wee cast anchor, and at 10 of the clocke in the night being very darke, was a false alarum given by the Watch of a partie comming, which made us all flye to our weapons, at last perceiving it was but one Boate, and they that were in it, crying out Friends from the Duke of Neuburg, else wee had shot them, who came for to have passage into England.

Next morning earely wee weyed anchor, and went part of the day in danger likewise, to Orsoy, the first Garrison Towne of the States, where we were stayed, and our Ship searched what wee carried, but at our

<66>

putting off, they gave us two Pieces of Ordnance; so from thence along by Rhineberg, against which there lay a man of Warre of the States, who saluted us with three Pieces; then by Buricksweasell, and a league further we cast anchor in the middle of the Rhyne, sayling this day but 4 leagues and a halfe, by reason of our stay at severall Toll places.

The next day earely in the morning, set sayle, and sayled downe by Rhees, Emmericke, and by Schenck-Schants, which is now new built and well fortified againe, where wee left the Rhyne and that on our right hand, and went downe in a deepe River called the Wall, by Nimmegen a faire Towne, seated on the East side of the Rhyne on a hanging Hill, where the Governour of the Towne, Sonne to one of the States, came forth and tendered his service to his Excellence. In which Towne there dyed this Summer

12.000 people of the Plague, but now thankes be to God, it is almost ceased: from thence, passing by severall Redoubt-Houses built at every halfe league, in which there lyeth a Watch continually to keepe the River, passing along untill wee came to the fourth House; where, for all wee told them it was an English Ambassador, shot foure or five Pieces at us, and mist some of us very narrowly; whereupon wee cast anchor, and lay in the middle of the Rhyne, but could not certainly learne who they were, saylling this day seaven leagues.

December the 8. in the morning, wee set sayle and went to Teill, being but two leagues, and could not passe any further for yee, but sayled in great danger

<67>

thither of splitting our Ship by the violent force of it, which caused us to stay there three dayes, untill we heard there might be a passage cut over the Rhyne at Viana; departed thither upon little Sledges, on Sunday the eleventh of December, and passed over great quantities of yce, through Burem, where the Prince of Orange hath a faire Castle, thence to Culenburg, and so to Viana to Bed, travelling with much labour some on foot, others by the sledges this day 6 leagues, where Sir Ferdinando Curie, an English Gentleman, entertained his Excellence that night, the Towne is very pleasantly seated upon the East side of the Rhyne, and their rest thinges in it, are Flowers, for there was a Tulip-roote sold lately for 340 pounds, as Sir Ferdinando informed his Excellence.

The next morning, wee tooke Boate and crossed over the River though with much danger and difficulty in the wet, the winde and tyde contrary, being got ashorm, went to Vtrecht where we lay that night, which was but 2 leagues, and where there then dyed of the Plague 80 a weeke, but a little before 300; from thence to Leyden next day to Bed, travelling very late, and eight leagues this day; where some of the Princes the Queene of Bohemia's Sonnes, were at Schoole, whom his Excellence presently visited, and there met with some Gentlemen, which the Queene had sent to meet his Excellence, and two of her Coaches to fetch him to the Hague.

The next day before his Excell[ence] went away, he viewed the chiefe things of note in the Towne, as the Vniversities, the Anatomie Schoole, which before we had

<68>

bot leysure to see, and from thence after dinner to the Hague, which was but 3 leagues, being Wednesday the 14th day of December, and their Christmas Eve [=24.12.].

Thus leaving his Excellence at the Hague, I went for Amsterdam that famous Citie, first by Waggon to Harlem, which was five leagues, where I lay that night, being a very well built Towne, the next day to the Citie it selfe, which was three leagues, passing all the way upon a Cawsey, by Harlem-Meare on my right hand, and the River Tey on the left, and entred in at Harlem-Port, and past through all the new Towne, and over three large Graufts, Princes, Keasers, and the Heares Grauft, these Streets be three Quarters of an English mile in length, two hundreth paces in bredth, having an even row of stately beautifull Buildings, and Trees planted the whole length of the Graufts side, and so into the old Towne, which is not of so stately a building, but the whole Citie is built upon Piles in the water, and a great Channell runneth through every Street for the Marchants ships to sayle to their doores, their Exchange is built much like unto that in London, both beneath and above, but that it wants a little in breadth, with water running under it, there is a very large building called the Weishouse [=Waisenhaus], wherein all poore Children, Fatherlesse, or of decayed Parents, are there maintained and brought up, and there is now at this present time 800 all clad alike, the one side of their garments Blacke and the other Red; there is likewise foure Hospitals adjoyning one unto another, for Men and Women to be severed each from other, the East and West Indian Houses, two

<69>

rare Builings and curious within, and many other delightfull things to please the eye, heere I stayed two dayes; and on Saturday the 17. day of December, at 5 of the clocke at night, tooke a Scute [=Schute] drawne by a Horse, and went up a River along by the side of the Cawsey; than I passed downe on before to Harlem, and there at 10 of the clocke in the Evening tooke a Waggon, and travailed all night to the Hague, which was five leagues; but ferried over the Rhyne at two in the morning, and got thither by 8 of the clocke; where wee stayed Eight dayes, and the most part of the time was spent at the Queenes Court, and the rest in visites, betweene the Prince of Orange, the States, and three Ambassadors which were there; as Monsieur Charnesse from France, Seignior Carmerarius for the Swedes, the Venetian Ambassador, and the Count of Culenburg; but hearing our Ship was come, his Excellence tooke leave of the Queene at 10 of the clocke at night, and came away next morning being Wednesday, the one and twentieth of December, and Prince Maurice along with him to Keswicke, where the Prince of Orange hath a House, which his Excellence viewed, and then the Prince taking leave returned backe againe, and his Excellence rode on forward in her Majesties Coach to Delft where he dined, in which Towne there are as many Bridges as Dayes in the yeare, and so many Channels and Streets, where Boates doe passe up and downe, and one common Passage under a Church-yard, under which wee did passe, from thence by a Scute to

Rotterdam, where we lay, which is from the Hague five leagues, untill that the

<70>

winde served us, and then on Saturday being the 24. of December – and Christmas Eve by our stile – at a 11 of the clocke in the night, tooke Boates and went to our Ship, sayling first through Magan Sluce to Helver-Sluce, where our Ship called the Garland did ride at anchor, and about 3 in the afternoone set sayle, and sayled over the Barre, having a Pilate sayling before us with a Lanthorne on the top of his Mast, sounding for the depth all the way; and the next day at twelue of the clocke cast Anchor in the Dounes, and there rid and could not land for the rough-nesse of the Sea, untill Tuesday morning the 27. of December, and then landed at Deale, and from thence by Poast to Canterbury, and so to Sittinburne to bed.

The next day in the morning earely to Gravesend, and there tooke water for London; where on the way, my Right Honourable Lady met his Excellence, who exchanged Barges, and there she entertained him with a Banquet, and so earely the next morning, went to Hampton Court to his Majesty.

FINIS.